How to Thread a Needle

poems by

Miriam Weinstein

Finishing Line Press
Georgetown, Kentucky

How to Thread a Needle

Copyright © 2022 by Miriam Weinstein
ISBN 978-1-64662-955-8 First Edition
All rights reserved under International and Pan-American Copyright Conventions. No part of this book may be reproduced in any manner whatsoever without written permission from the publisher, except in the case of brief quotations embodied in critical articles and reviews.

ACKNOWLEDGMENTS

Deepest appreciation to the publishers who originally published these, or another version, of the poems below:

"A nod to poems unwritten," *Portages Magazine*
"At the supermarket" (formerly "Abundance"), *Poems of Hope and Reassurance*
"In my hand," forthcoming, *St. Paul Almanac*
"How to thread a needle," *Rag Queen*
"Long underwear and a lady's slipper," *Oakwood Magazine*
"So much depends upon leaves," *Constellate Literary Journal*
"The allure of late summer," *Martin Lake Journal*
"The muse," *Oakwood Magazine*
"Today—we're writing this poem together," *Talking Stick*, Volume 25
"When I'm gone," *Blotterature*

For their ongoing inspiration and advice, a heartfelt thank you to Jude Nutter, Margaret Hasse, and Thomas R. Smith, my mentors for more than a decade.

My deepest appreciation to members of the Ginger Poetry Workshop and the Foreword Poetry Program, especially, to the memory of the fine poet James Bettendorf and the insightful critiques he shared.

Publisher: Leah Huete de Maines
Editor: Christen Kincaid
Cover Art: Miriam Weinstein
Author Photo: Laurie Erickson Photography
Cover Design: Elizabeth Maines McCleavy

Order online: www.finishinglinepress.com
also available on amazon.com

Author inquiries and mail orders:
Finishing Line Press
PO Box 1626
Georgetown, Kentucky 40324
USA

Table of Contents

A strand of pearls 1
At the supermarket 2
Ode to two "M"s 3
Collected poems 4
In my hand 5
Ars poetica 6
Meditation on a walk by Lake Harriet 7
One thing I know 8
The muse 9
A ring, a desire, a memory 10
There are things I won't write in ink 12
The body remembers 13
Unwinding 14
It's not a straight shot 15
Woman wandering 16
Constellations 17
Illusions of permanence 18
Long underwear and a lady's slipper 19
Ode to a spring day 20
As if it will always shine 21
Today—this poem we're writing together 23
The allure of late summer 24
The surprise 25
So much depends upon leaves 26
How I learned to thread a needle 27
A new year 28
When I'm gone 29
A nod to poems unwritten 30
How solitary 31
Horizons 32

Dedicated to my mother Frances Lipton Weinstein
and
to my mentors
Margaret Hasse, Jude Nutter, Thomas R. Smith

A strand of pearls

It could be any of many moments when you realize
you, too, are vulnerable. Before this, your life,

a strand of pearls, felt arranged in a predetermined
order: each pearl, next to the others, formed inside

an oyster for this very purpose. The luster of individual
pearls reflected off others. Perfectly strung,

they became a strand to fasten behind your neck
and settle on bare skin above a scalloped collar.

You felt the strand would provide protection, always,
like a talisman. Then, the thread tattered, pearls scattered,

and tumbled out of sight. You gathered a few
before they disappeared, and wrapped

your palm around them. Unsettled as the gems
that rolled away, you realized that strand of pearls

was lent to you though you acted as if you owned it.
The remnants will be used, at best, for a pair of earrings

or a ring. Something to wear when you go out
to face all that you know is unpredictable.

Some pearls have rolled into wedged places
between your kitchen wall and the floor boards,

places you never noticed before you knelt
trying to reclaim them.

At the supermarket

bold, bright sunflowers stare into my face,
bouquets of alstromeria with lily-like petals
painted mauve and lemon-yellow.
Hot pink or twilight blue daisies vie for attention.
Colors arc into the produce section where fruit
cascades from displays. Heaps of mangos,
varieties of melons, apples and oranges.

I imagine my grandmother as a young girl,
resting for a moment by a brook outside
her *shtetl* in Romania.
It is an October day much like today.
The heat of summer, a memory, a balmy
breeze swirls her skirt as she sits and savors
an apple snatched from under a tree.

Who knows how long this piece of fruit lay
on the ground before it was found, small
and withered. It doesn't matter.
She enjoys each bite. The tip of her bare
toes touch the water, sunshine
warms her back.

Ode to two "M"s

Mountain ranges
on either end
of my name

twin guardians
over a valley
of vowels

a rolling hill
in between. Lips held
together hum. Strum.
Drum an ever endless
sound. Ancient music
making melodies
echo from peak
to peak.

Call it
the first
speech—"em"
murmuring
in the mouth.

My life in your cradle,
my body in your arms
double "em" dreaming.

Collected poems
after Linda Pastan

They take you through my life, one poem
at a time. Memory's markers, unpredictable
and selective, I invent to fill gaps.
Poems in cardboard file boxes: boxes
sold flattened, three for five dollars, easy
to assemble. Arranged, now, in no
particular order. Short phrases repeat
again and again across pages.
Love's rapture and rupture
mixed in the poems: my ponytail secured
in a band, my daughter's curly, black locks
in a bag. And my father's thick hair
with dried bits of a boutonnière,
his individual white hairs
almost glued to a few poems,
the mass of hair that fell from his head
after chemotherapy. Dead, more
than a decade and a half, Father looms
over the pages, touches each poem
with his long, manicured finger tips.
At 92, mother stands nearby still questioning,
correcting, forgetting: truth is not in the details.
Father's desk, now in my office; rarely used
though rough drafts fill the top drawer.
I remember him sitting at work. He looks up
and welcomes me into his room.

In my hand

Today, from the top shelf of my closet, I retrieve a large box
of photos. Years compress and expand. Photos ten and fifteen
years old mingle with photos taken twenty-five years ago

of a family vacation. Cobblestone streets, and a street market
in Mexico, a plain wooden playground, my daughter swinging
from monkey bars. Much like the iPhone video her husband

sent last week, their seven-year-old daughter, her legs
swinging to fill the frame, proudly shimmies closer
to the camera. A video runs in my head—

my granddaughter as a toddler sways from a jungle gym
then I see images of her at four and seven years old moving
along bars. I continue to shuffle through piles of photos,

one comes into focus. My daughter at the State Capitol,
her first choice, a tour of this majestic building on her sixth
birthday. Hand in mine, I remember how she tilted

her head to take in details of artwork on the ceiling. How
she called her name, again and again, delight on her face
as she listened to the echo of her voice under the round dome.

Home after our tour, she slept curled in the recliner, her legs
in lavender tights stretched over the arm, her feet wrapped
in boot-slippers.   Now, here—in my hand,

a photo pulled from a haphazard heap—my daughter asleep
exactly as I remember. Photos, some in plastic and paper
envelopes, some held together with rubber bands.

A medley of memories in my mind as we dash to the swing
set and, for a moment, are all six years old, pumping
higher and higher our legs

    extend   in a race to touch the sky.

Ars poetica

This is no catch and release sport. When you feel
a tug on your line, brace yourself and begin—

reel that catch in with all the strength you've got.
Do you really know when another will come along?

Don't risk losing this one. Remember the pleasure
in scaling that catch with your finest knife, in lifting

bones from flesh, in grilling meat until it flakes
with a touch of your fork. Done, your catch

may nourish others. Don't wonder about this now.
Focus on your catch. Focus on the guts.

Meditation on a walk by Lake Harriet

Sunlight glistens against the lake as clouds
gather in the west, waves roll to shore,
and ducks rummage in the water.
Shadows dance on the ground, on the grass,
in the gully. Take this moment
for what it offers. Even cans washed
ashore shine and water glows laced with algae.
Light flits, this moment, through trees and mingles
with the breeze. Thankful for its cooling fingers,
thankful, too, for what it carries away.

Take the breeze.

One thing I know

One thing I know for certain—I love to watch
my dog napping in the sun on a spring day.

She spreads herself out, rolls on her side, and hugs
the hardwood floor until her body is almost flat. Flat

as a blintz in a hot frying pan. The first and the second
bubbles pop and it's time to flip the dough and brown

the other side. That's another thing I know—
how to make a blintz. How to mix and measure

the flour, milk, and egg. But back to my dog
breathing steadily in and out as she sleeps

during her mid-afternoon nap. Her breath
like the rhythm of waves rolling gently

to shore, sweeping aside a layer of sand
and then placing it down as if never disturbed.

My dog's sleeping feet shake as she readies herself
to run through her dream. Maybe she is with me

in her dream and we are about to begin a great game
of *go chase*. A game she could play for hours. No sense

of time or pending appointments to preoccupy her.
I would give anything to be, for one short afternoon,

my dog.
But, no, not for more than one short afternoon.

The muse

Sweeping into my chamber unexpectedly, her gifts
rain down, and I soak up these offerings
like a soldier welcomes peace after a long battle.

To she who bestows: How can I possibly show
my gratitude? During her sojourn, should I lie
with her, forego sleep, become

a handmaiden to her every need: burning
incense, lighting candles, singing praises?

I am certain she needs air to breath, oxygen
to fuel her fire—I will not hover.

I walk outside following the creek,
sheltered by willows, I listen to waters caught
for a moment by a cluster of rocks, then released.

The trill of song birds guides me, until, heeding
the raucous warning of a crow, I leave my refuge.

The air is filled with the melody of a gardener
humming as she trims rosebushes. I pause

then return the greeting. My gaze is held
by her deep brown eyes.

Did the wistful scent of autumn roses soften
my reserve?

A reservoir opens before me.

A ring, a desire, a memory

A shop assistant attentive to my wishes selects
rings to consider, all the while commenting
on my coloring, my clothing, my jewelry.

She watches as I slip rings on and off, extending
my hand and tilting it to catch the jewel in sunlight.
She notices the subtle comparison I make between

the ring I return to repeatedly and my ring. Theirs:
a sapphire gemstone resting on a thick, artfully
designed platinum band. Mine: white gold,

two etched swirls circling around it. Not tarnished,
not sparkling either. She asks, *Would you like,
your ring polished?* Clever assistant, she knows once

back on my finger, the store's fine jewel will enhance
my ring; lead me to discover their sapphire gem
was made for me.

...

The sapphire gem was made for me. I peer
in the glass case at jewels designed from precious
metals and gemstones. *Handmade jewelry,*

the assistant remarks, *has a soul.* I think of ancient
human ornaments: shells, bones, teeth, and berries,
pieces of stone strung on strands of fiber fashioned

into necklaces and earrings. *Handmade jewelry
has a soul*, she repeats, as I hand her my credit card.
Will I request this ring remain on my finger

at my burial? Primitive appeasement and offering
to the gods, small price for the doors of heaven
to open. How we gather and cling to the beauties

of this world. Then, moments later leaving the shop,
I catch the jewel sparkling in sunlight. Unbidden,
I wonder, which daughters' hand? My desire—

this ring remind her of me, a cherished gemstone
to strengthen that which holds us. A fabric as easily
frayed by life as silver is tarnished by air.

. . .

Frayed by life, tarnished by air. Too fancy
for daily wear, I place the ring in my jewelry box.
A few treasured pieces surround it. A favorite,

the Order of the Coif key my father carried
in his pocket every day. His name engraved
on the back. Each time I hold the key

in my hand, I hold his image. Home after work,
he removed it from his pocket as I clutched his leg.
Opening the clasp where the gold key hung

from a chain attached to a belt loop, I watched him
set it on the dresser. I remember circling around
his legs, inhaling the fabric of his woolen trousers;

then circling again, one last time.

There are things I won't write in ink

Infidelity, the depth of the sea, unfathomable to me.
Yesterday, blue pierced the clouds. Today, gray.
Impervious gray. Denied, relief of rain

to clean and calm. I press for details. Details
I will not put to the page. Words in ink on paper
fall flat. Partial truths, incomplete answers.

The line of our circle uncurls into points
that threaten to impale. Hollow sound echoes
through the house. A voice, once full, falls

flat like words on paper. Words—

The body remembers

the weight of your hand on my waist while we slept.
The body remembers twirling under your arm,
swirling away until the rhythm of the music
pulled us together and you held me,
the timbre of your voice touching my ear.
The body remembers your shape against mine,
our legs intertwined. I vow to forget—
but the body remembers.

Unwinding

When you built cages, late last autumn, around our rosebushes
were you, already, thinking of her? Carefully you secured

chicken wire to the ground and then formed a bed
of dry leaves around the stems.

Today—chilly in May—I loosen the cages, unwind
the wire. Leaves stand like turrets covering the plants.

I raise them one at a time while thinking of you. You:
rosebush lover, garden steward. In a book you left behind,

I learn about rosebushes, about their reputation for being difficult,
about their forgiving nature. Soak roots deeply, occasionally.

Avoid brief, shallow waterings. Your handwritten note
at the bottom of the page: one tablespoon

of Epsom salts in a gallon of water encourages healthy canes.
You often soaked in salts—care for some ache or another—

did you also, each spring, mix the salts with water and drench
the roots? So much I never noticed. Long days stretching

into months, into years as you tended flower beds alone.
Many a Saturday our late afternoon date missed, you

leaning over plants. Now you, my turret, you left,
but your essence still winds around me. And I remember,

more than once you called the garden your mistress.

It's not a straight shot

down my laundry chute, remodeling jobs changed
the configuration. Plumbing or air-conditioning pipes,

I don't remember which, now run along its walls.
Awake between 2:15 and 3:30 A.M., I empty

and fold the contents of my yellow laundry hamper.
Brown and beige towels, stacked in an uneven pile,

remind me of the rock formations north
of my hometown. Before settling back into bed

with a book, I tuck my top sheet under my mattress
and, at each end, form hospital corners. Thumbing

through a poetry anthology on grief and gratitude,
I find nothing that holds me to the final stanza. I make

a mental list and drift to sleep. Dreaming down
one side of my life a hidden room opens to a circus

show in the center of a secondhand store. My ex
rarely visits my dreams, but when she does

I'm not home.

This is not a dream. Two years to the day after
her exit, I open the main floor door of the laundry

chute and find her blouse dangling like a broken
arm. No amount of tugging releases it.

My son-in-law dislodges the dirty blue blouse
and drops it in the trash.

Woman wandering

I am a question mark unlocking doors,
        a catalogue of inquires;
I am a map without boundaries,
        a bareback bronco ride.
I am a frozen field of ripe corn,
        a snowstorm in July.
I am a cactus flowering in the night,
        a stream of tears on the desert floor;
I am a thread binding truths.

I am mercy with my imploring palm—
        a beggar at the door.

Constellations

Through branches of the maple, a solitary
lamp illuminates the darkness.

A writer burning with inspiration? A neighbor
returning home from work? Yards apart

stars glow in galaxies
of their own.

Illusions of permanence

An emerald green, silicone potholder, its surface
of blunt teeth-like bumps at the ready, hangs
gaping. Outside, the fledged house sparrows pursue
their parents. Wings fluttering
earnestly, their beaks, toothless mouths
hanging open, asserting their will to survive.

I think of the woman standing by the freeway
entrance yesterday holding a sign: *Homeless.
Desperate. Please help.* Her graying hair pulled back
in a tidy bun. Home. A handy illusion of permanence
when you have one. Today, on the public radio web page
a fluffy red heart pierced by an arrow floats above
the city skyline with a request for submissions.
What everyday sights and sounds of your city

make it "home"? At dusk, we watch a mallard drake
circle near the sandy shore of Lake Harriet, iridescent
emerald head and a white band of feathers encircling
his neck; he circles again, then plunges his head
in the water, dark stub of a tail and yellow legs
in the air. The setting sun wraps a blanket
around us. I could lose myself

in your emerald eyes, and always feel I am home.

Long underwear and a lady's slipper
   after Margaret Hasse

We return to spring
leaving winter woolens and layers of snow
over ice. Back from the season
of darkness, of sunbeams held by shadows.
Back from long evening solitude.

While scilla scatters across the ground, winter
still burrows beneath my skin. I stand, arms crossed
and eyes wary, as lilacs beg windows to open.
Bleeding hearts hang and violets multiply
in gardens and on grass. Now maple seeds drift
to the ground searching
for soil. And, now,

I peel off my sweater, unbolt the heavy door.
I come back to spring:
to water surging in swollen brooks,
to lilies blooming in the night,
to sun falling from lapis skies.

Ode to a spring day

On this day heavy with moisture a breeze
between showers shakes droplets from branches.
Violets carpet my neighbor's lawn in blue,
and dandelions in all stages of growth—some
with bold yellow caps, others, gone to seed—play
with memory; of how, in a circle of friends
I held my hand high to wave their downy tops

in every direction.

In a neglected flower bed, wild columbine mingles
with daffodils and tulips, pink fists dot crabapple
trees, the edge of each blossom traced
with a delicate red line—and I'm running,
running across the lawns of childhood, waiting
to hear my friends shriek
ready or not as clenched buds open

and raise their palms to the sky.

As if it will always shine

Today, a cardinal announces his presence from the top of a lilac
hedge, sunshine accentuating vivid reds. Juncos peck at a pile
of seed hulls, search the mound for food, bright white
underbellies visible as they tilt their heads.

And the sun shines as if it will always shine on our lives—
mine and the birds. Today, I talk to the sun: Melt the snow, I say,
melt it all today. Pull up the crocus flowers ready to emerge
from their bulbs, pull up all early spring flowers that sing
to the world. Give me the hope held in spring.

Earlier, I awoke to the same news I've heard my entire life.
The U.N. Secretary-General, Ban Ki-moon says: North Korea's
nuclear threats are not a game and the current crisis has gone
too far. I listened today

and as a young girl. Air raid sirens tested every week, I practiced
drills at school with classmates. It was easy to see
Billy didn't have a chance, his arms and legs too long to scrunch
under his wooden school desk. Mom, a volunteer block organizer,
contacted each neighbor to discuss their assigned evacuation route.

So many years of my young life spent sure the enemy's bomb
pointed at everything I loved. At bedtime, Mom comforted me
patting my back. During the day, she had a mission: Door-to-door
she talked with neighbors to help them feel prepared. I never knew

until last year. The night we talked about life during the Cold War
she said, *Remember the elderly couple next door?* We're not
leaving our home, *they told me*, we will die here.

Once I saw a Kirtland's warbler perched in a jack pine: gray
with a bold yellow chest, and a ring of white around its eyes.
Called the "bird of fire" because its survival depends
on natural burning in the forest where it nests.
Fires extinguished regularly by humans and our needs.

Meanwhile, politicians test each other: spit words and gesture like bullies on a playground. Today, the sun shines as if it will always shine on our lives.

Today—this poem we're writing together

A derailment in Wisconsin—18,000 gallons
of ethanol spilled in the Mississippi. In the distance
bald eagles soaring, plunging into this bulge in the river
called Lake Pepin.

Gasoline. How we love it.

Ethanol. Crude oil. Crossing our country on rails built
for old freight trains. Winding past farms. Fields.
Whistle-stop towns. Cutting through the heart
of our cities.

Later—another derailment—another spill.
Crude oil in a different river. *Nothing more than an accident,*
the investigators say shaking their heads, lowering their eyes
as if in prayer.

The allure of late summer

Blossoms sway in the breeze, tease
A kaleidoscope of butterflies
Come, August offspring
The ancient courtship of flower and flyer

A kaleidoscope of butterflies
Tongues unravel to sip sweet nectar
The ancient courtship of flower and flyer
Aflutter over phlox, Joe-Pye weed, aster, coreopsis

Tongues unravel to sip sweet nectar
The allure of late summer
Aflutter over phlox, Joe-Pye weed, aster, coreopsis
The marvel of metamorphosis

Caterpillar to chrysalis to butterfly
Seeds of milkweed germinate
The marvel of metamorphosis
Monarchs glide in the garden

Seeds of milkweed germinate
Clusters migrate in waves along a primordial path
Monarchs glide in the garden
Silken wings woven with wonder lace the air

Clusters migrate in waves along a primordial path
Beckoned, butterflies descend
Silken wings woven with wonder lace the air
Ripples of orange and black, specks of white

Beckoned, butterflies descend
Blossoms sway in the breeze, tease
Ripples of orange and black, specks of white
Come, August offspring

The surprise

of that moment when,
enveloped by birch, the road arcs
and the trees fade away.
Then, around the bend,
the forest appears
again, trees swaying
in and out of sight
for miles,
a touch of blue
and white visible
between boughs—
the lake or sky—
clouds or waves undulate
in the distance, and you dream

of planting yourself—Here.

Was the allure of the leaves
an invitation or did branches beckon?

You slide between trees and take root.

So much depends upon leaves

So many leaves—what did I expect mid-November? As soon
as I pressure my daughter into raking them, it rains
that evening. What's left on the the ground, a damp and soggy

mess and then, dry in the morning, with one strong gust, more
wind-blown-into-my-yard leaves conceal the grass. Depending
upon whom I watch or what I read, I'm left confused about

leaves. Neighbors make a ruckus with their leaf blowers,
intent to leave not one behind. An article on the internet
encourages readers not to rake leaves, advises:

*leaves provide benefits to the environment. Placed over flower
beds, mulched and let to lie, leaves protect plants and supply
nutrients.* Squished into a rusty, old red wheelbarrow—

several bags filled with leaves. I cart them to the curb,
remembering the October day my daughter, tiny at two, plunked
down on a pile of leaves, pure bliss across her face as she threw

leaves and more leaves into the air, her head tilted to the sky,
she watched leaves tumble to the ground. Leaves covered her legs,
her torso, almost covered her entire body.   The beauty

of autumn leaves glazing the grass, the day drenched in sunshine
before what we didn't yet know, thirty years ago, would be
an evening of wind and rain and in the morning,

we'd wake to fields of snow.

How I learned to thread a needle

I don't remember her teaching me how to thread
a needle. Yet I see her today—a basket by her side
filled with spools of many colors, buttons
of many shapes, snaps of several sizes—a length
of thread in hand, she places it in her mouth
to moisten, then with her fingers forms
a perfect point she will easily
insert into the eye of the needle.

She squints, focuses on that almost invisible spot,
pokes the thread through the needle, takes the two
loose ends and twists them into a knot. Dozens
of pins pierce the surface of a cherry-red
pincushion, packets of binding and measuring
tape, steel-gray pinking shears, and a pair
of fabric scissors crowd her sewing basket.
I don't remember

Mother teaching me how to thread a needle,
how to sew on a button, how to hem a skirt,
but I watched her when I was young. And I watch
her now, as she navigates her nineties, pulling
threads from the past, creating a pattern
for the present—spools of many colors,
a decorative button here, a snap there, a zipper
along the side—open at the top.

A new year

Aspire to
bend like a willow on a windy day,
curve
deeply, and
enter that unfamiliar landscape in front of you without
fear. There,
germinate seeds of
hope and water them with optimism for tomorrow. Be
impetuous—picnic on an ice pond, zipline over treetops—and reserve
judgement.
Keep
laughter nearby opening it often like a favorite book. Keep
moments fluid, *never* uttering
never. Fill days with
open
peaceful
quiet
reflection. Then
surrender:
trust in the path you have chosen, raise an
umbrella of sustenance over your
vision, resist temptation to
wander from your task. And be mindful,
xenophobia includes the stranger within.
You: the proprietress of now. Now, before life
zeros during the stillness before dawn.

When I'm gone

Some day
I might return to be held
the way pages of a book
cradle a bookmark.

That soft space
between your arms
was what I liked best.

Remember me

when that bookmark
slips unexpectedly
and falls in your lap.

A nod to poems unwritten

There are poems unwritten in the drawers of my mind,
poems unformed, incomplete phrases lying out of order—
when did trouble find…how hard it… Phrases
like the would-be forest that attempts to take over
my yard where seedlings struggle to survive and dwarf
a burning bush now spreading its branches over
what I call weeds; where each morning I tether
my puppy to a tree and pull at weeds
while she sniffs and searches.
How much of life is rooted out unformed, how much
remains unfinished, how every life will end, and
how most break off mid—

How solitary

the life of a spider,
how many hours filled
with filling space,
with weaving
expansions,
with designing
additions
and then,
how many
more hours filled
with the long wait
for that single moment:
the heft of a fatal fall.

Horizons
    after Rebecca McClanahan

Needing my family still, I come
when I can, this time to the northern most
shore of Green Bay where, for a week, we share
meals crowded around tables pushed together
to make room for thirteen chairs.
Floorboards squeak with the rhythm of steps between
the kitchen and the dining room. Forks scrape plates.
Parents cajole children: *finish the green beans,*
Grandma's pie for dessert. Remember
the cherries we picked
yesterday?

The baby, barely one, at one end of the table; Mother,
ninety-two this week, at the other. She claps
her hands when the baby circles the table, reaches
arms out offering her lap; he settles
for a moment, but his papa is quick to scoop
him up when he whimpers. Meals pattern the days,
otherwise, they drift with unspoken memories
of Father coloring the spaces
between us. I go off on my own, and later listen
to my great-niece, how she taught her cousins to ride
the waves on an inner tube, how on a hike along
the rugged coast of Lake Michigan
she found stone monuments.

The afternoon I left, the family divided
into three: one group off to a sandy beach, another
off on errands, and me—I was heading west.
Each dusk we'd shared the sunset as it lingered over
the water, waves lapping to meet the sky. The only
sound: the baby's babble taking us into another
day as we'd waited, together, imagining
how the sun might color the sky
beyond our horizon.

Miriam Weinstein's poems are published in several anthologies: *A 21st Century Plague: Poetry from a Pandemic, Rocked By The Waters: Poems of Motherhood, Poems of Hope and Reassurance, Nuclear Impact: Broken Atoms in Our Hands, The Heart of All That Is: Reflections on Home,* and in journals including *Survivor Lit, New Verse News, Oakwood Magazine, Portages Magazine, Evening Street Review, Rag Queen, Indian River Review, Vita Brevis Press,* and *Plum Street Tavern*. Her first chapbook, *Twenty Ways of Looking,* was published by Finishing Line Press in 2016. *How to Thread A Needle* is the re-designed and edited version of a full-length manuscript that was shortlisted for the Concrete Wolf Press Louis Award. A self-taught photographer, her collection of black and white silver-prints has been exhibited in Minnesota and Wisconsin. Weinstein holds two Master of Education degrees, one in Family Life Education, the other in Adult Education, and a Bachelor of Arts degree in Dramatic Arts. She completed the Loft Literary Center's Apprenticeship Program in Poetry. Miriam lives in Minneapolis, Minnesota where she is an avid birdwatcher—in her backyard, while walking around city lakes, along Minnehaha Parkway and the Mississippi River.

www.ingramcontent.com/pod-product-compliance
Lightning Source LLC
LaVergne TN
LVHW041601070426
835507LV00011B/1235